ROMANTIC PIECES
for Alto Saxophone & Piano

Music Minus One

4143

SUGGESTIONS FOR USING THIS MMO EDITION

We have tried to create a product that will provide you an easy way to learn and perform these compositions with a full ensemble in the comfort of your own home. The following MMO features and techniques will help you maximize the effectiveness of the MMO practice and performance system:

Because it involves a fixed accompaniment performance, there is an inherent lack of flexibility in tempo. We have observed generally accepted tempi, and always in the originally intended key, but some may wish to perform at a different tempo, or to slow down or speed up the accompaniment for practice purposes; or to alter the piece to a more comfortable key. For maximum flexibility, you can purchase from MMO specialized CD players & recorders which allow variable speed while maintaining proper pitch, and vice versa. This is an indispensable tool for the serious musician and you may wish to look into purchasing this useful piece of equipment for full enjoyment of all your MMO editions.

We want to provide you with the most useful practice and performance accompaniments possible. If you have any suggestions for improving the MMO system, please feel free to contact us. You can reach us by e-mail at *info@musicminusone.com*.

Music Minus One

4143

CONTENTS

featuring Alyssa Hoffert, guest alto saxophonist playing 2nd Saxophone Part

ISBN 978-1-59615-770-5

FOREWORD

THIS ALBUM REPRESENTS A FINE COLLECTION of elegant classical masterpieces by such renowned composers as Gluck, Rachmaninov, and Schubert, combined with compositions by their living counterparts Morgan, Raman and Taylor. A "musical marriage" has been created on this album, combining works by some of history's greatest musical masters with contemporary prolific composers writing for the saxophone.

These timeless works highlight the tonal beauty, sonority, color, and expressive qualities inherent in the saxophone, which has the ability to sound at times like a mezzo-soprano, violinist, cellist, or flutist. A wide spectrum of tonal colors can be achieved if study of these various instruments, their compositions, and the classical style is embraced.

It is the obligation of orchestral saxophonists to not only study the saxophone masters that precede us, such as Rascher, Deffayet, Mule, and Abato (Abato can be heard on MMO 4112, 4114, 4116, 4118), but to learn also from these masters' musical inspirations, which include Heifetz, Rampal, du Pré, and Moffo, to name only a few.

Toscanini instructed his wind players that "you must put a drop of blood in each note," a philosophy that is embraced on this album. Each work allows the saxophonist's musical horizons to be expanded. Although the sheet music with "notes on the page" is provided, the performer must seek out what is not written. This is a life-long journey of self-expression which leads to a rewarding musical experience for both the performer and the audience.

ORPHÉE: SCÈNE DES CHAMPS-ÉLYSÉES
Christoph Willibald Ritter von Gluck
arr. Greg Banaszak (1991)

Our musical journey begins with a composition from 1762. "Scène des Champs-Élysées" is from Gluck's opera *Orpheo and Euridice*, and depicts Orpheus' journey to Hades, the realm of the dead, in search of his departed wife, Euridice. Gluck captures, in this music, a wealth of emotions for the performer and listener to absorb, experience, and indulge in.

Each phrase should initially be subdivided and worked on meticulously with a metronome, since the rhythms can be deceptively challenging. A term that I and others like to use is "rhythmic integrity," which is truly essential in capturing the creative elements within this work. I also suggest isolating all the grace notes in order to understand exactly how to execute them within the rhythmic parameters of the underlying flow of sixteenth notes in the piano accompaniment. All the ornamentation should be delicate and unobtrusive. Isolate the larger intervals and sing them first to help the lower notes speak clearly so they can be colored *"senza vibrato"* (without vibrato) before gracefully fading away.

Andante Amoroso
Brian Scott Taylor (2012)

Accomplished NYC pianist, conductor, musical director, and composer Brian Taylor shares his compositional talents with us, allowing the alto saxophonist to take on the role of a vocalist. Having appeared with Renee Fleming and Orpheus Chamber Orchestra on *Live from Lincoln Center* on PBS, Mr. Taylor offers the saxophonist a window into the expressive world so many vocalists enjoy and relish in. "Andante Amoroso" is a lyrical piece expressing unrequited love. Use of unresolved suspensions and undulating counter-melodies represent the bittersweet yearning found in the writings of Walt Whitman, which are the inspiration behind the music.

This piece should be approached as a "song without words," with each melodic phrase being played as if it were a heartfelt sentence, finding the hidden speech patterns in the rhythm of the melody. The quarter-note triplets, in particular, need to be played smoothly and with great ease. Meticulous focus must be given to the very first note, a concert D, which tends to be bright on the saxophone. In order to emulate the human voice, the saxophone must enter with the same sonority and color as a vocalist. Use of vibrato is a personal tool of expression, but once again should emulate a vocalist. The subtleties heard in this recording emerge from a long-term and ongoing study of the flexibility and nuances of great vocalists.

Consolation
David Morgan (2006)

Multi-talented composer and bassist David Morgan enjoys a rich and rewarding career as a successful classical and jazz artist. He has performed with and composed for today's leading jazz virtuosos, including Joe Lovano, Cedar Walton, Larry Coryell, and James Moody, to name a few. "Consolation" and "First Light" are originally part of Morgan's three-movement composition for alto saxophone and strings entitled "Three Vignettes," and can be heard on Centaur Records (*Romances for Saxophone and Orchestra* CRC 2889/90).

"Consolation" is a slow, lyrical piece in which a very simple folk-like melody gains poignancy through a variety of reharmonizations. It addresses several skills essential to enhancing and strengthening the ability to play long melodies at slower tempos. It is important to hear the note prior to playing it—this approach can be applied to any and all styles of music, and has served me well in my career. As the melody unwinds and the harmony slowly becomes more complex, the subtleties of articulation, vibrato, and dynamic expansion must be applied within every phrase. Although I have recorded and globally performed this thought-provoking piece for many years, it was only prior to this recording that I began to embrace what string players and vocalists use regularly—the *portamento*, or "falling," between certain notes. It simply feels natural for me to do so at this point in my career. One must be very cautious in emulating a *portamento*, since it must be within the bounds of meticulous intonation, and cannot have any hint of sounding jazz-influenced.

First Light (Tango)
David Morgan (2006)

"First Light" is influenced by South American musical traditions, and, in the composer's own words, is evocative of "the way the world looks and feels when the sun is first starting to come up on a summer morning." A lilting *rumba* rhythm is maintained throughout, as melodies and countermelodies bounce back and forth between the two alto saxophones and piano.

This piece was arranged specifically for this MMO album. In this arrangement, Morgan allows the two saxophonists to enjoy the parts that would normally be played by the orchestra. Deceptively difficult melodies and countermelodies are skillfully intertwined between the two alto saxophones, without one having a dominant role at any point. Specific care should be given to playing the sixteenth quarter-note triplet figures, which have a natural tendency to rush. Impeccable intonation is paramount in achieving true artistic expression in any performance involving two like wind instruments. In addition to understanding the tendencies inherent in all saxophones (regardless of specific make, year or model), the performers must achieve a high level of blend, dynamic control, and astute listening in order to reach a successful performance. I suggest listening to the music of South America, as well as to saxophonists such as Stan Getz and Paquito D'Rivera, percussionist Chano Pozo, and trumpet legend/bandleader Dizzy Gillespie to give the performance of this work stylistic authenticity. First the performers, then ultimately the audience, must be lured to move their bodies as one naturally does when rhythm and harmony are combined in one strong and enjoyable musical presence.

Aria
Subaram Raman (2006)

Hailed by world-renowned composer Maestro Krzysztof Penderecki as "one of today's truly gifted composers," Subaram Raman enjoys composing in several styles and genres, representing a rare ability to balance traditional composition styles with his own very creative, thought-provoking and vibrant voice. His "Aria," arranged here for alto saxophone and piano (originally with string orchestra, which also can be heard on my *Romances* CD, CRC2889/90), pays partial homage to composer Eugene Bozza. The lush harmonies and dramatic melodies heard throughout this piece are used in conscious opposition to what Raman believes to be a modern saxophone repertoire that has been dominated by objectivity. His use of color on the alto saxophone in a *pianissimo* setting, verging on *niente*, was inspired by hearing a performance of mine in Los Angeles. Raman's vision was to create melody while retaining the lyrical and vocal characteristics of the saxophone.

Raman's "Aria" gives saxophonists on opportunity to hone their creative skills while incorporating a tone that is pure and clear, like fine crystal. It is helpful to find a natural dynamic "comfort zone" prior to working on this piece, and not to immediately try to play at a "ppp" level. Playing too softly too soon only creates tension in the embouchure, hands, upper body, etc... many unnecessary problems to avoid. I suggest first imaging this beautiful melody without any dynamics and playing it with a pure tone such as that of clarinet virtuosos Robert Marcellus and Vincent Abato, respectively. This will allow a sense of warmth to emerge within this gorgeous piece, and facilitate exploring a vibrato that grows out of almost nothing into a full, dark, rich vibrato, while simultaneously applying dynamic contrast. Repeating each note ten to fifteen times at a *pianissimo* dynamic level, using a mirror to ensure that the embouchure is strong, centered, and controlled, is also very helpful. The goal, whether in a duo setting or as a soloist with full orchestra, is to "fill the hall, yet be as soft as a whisper!"

Vocalise, Op. 34, no 14
Sergei Rachmaninov

A *vocalise* is a composition for voice without text. Since the saxophone has frequently been described as one of the instruments most closely sounding like the human voice, it is quite fitting that an arrangement of Sergei Rachmaninov's *Vocalise* is present in this collection. The richness of this beautiful, haunting melody is stunning. Rachmaninov's musical style may be characterized as sincere expression combined with a skillful understanding of late Romantic compositional techniques; it is a combination particularly well suited to the sound and expressive qualities of the saxophone. (My orchestral arrangement of this work can be heard on Centaur Records' *Saxophone Concertos*, CRC #2400.)

First and foremost, while studying this work, the saxophonist must strip any aspect of vibrato and play the melody with the use of a tuner—I even suggest two tuners: the first drones any pitch (tonic, the third , fifth etc...), and another tuner monitors intonation by watching the needle. Only when the intonation is secure should the slightest use of vibrato be applied, always with precise intonation in mind. Vibrato, again, is a personal statement... mezzo-soprano Anna Moffo is a source of artistry and inspiration for all in this regard.

Serenade ("Ständchen" from *Schwanengesang*)
Franz Schubert

Our musical journey concludes with Franz Schubert's famous "Serenade," or "Ständchen," which is part of Schubert's *Schwanengesang*, a collection published after his early death in 1828. "Ständchen" remains one of the most loved of all his songs. It was originally composed in 1826 as an alto solo with male chorus, and then was subsequently rearranged for female voices only. It is now performed in many different instrumental versions.

This melody needs to simply be allowed to play itself, which is easier said than done. Some of the dynamics and articulations in my arrangement differ from those for various other instruments, in order to be "saxophone specific." It is important not to be overbearing in any way, and to control the saxophone's tendency to sometimes overpower the piano and to be misperceived as playing insensitively. Many arrangements, including this one, are derived from pieces composed before the saxophone was even invented, and they should be performed with stylistic integrity!

—*Greg Banaszak*
June 2012

Alto Saxophone

Orphée
Scène des Champs-Élysées

Christoph Willibald Ritter von Gluck
arr. G. Banaszak (1991)

note: 'f' indicates fork F♯, 'd1' indicates palm D, '5' indicates 1 & 5 fingering

Alto Saxophone

Andante Amoroso

Brian Taylor

Alto Saxophone

Consolation
for Alto Saxophone and Piano

David Morgan

Alto Saxophone I

First Light
(Tango)

David Morgan

Alto Saxophone

to Greg Banaszak

Aria

Subaram Raman

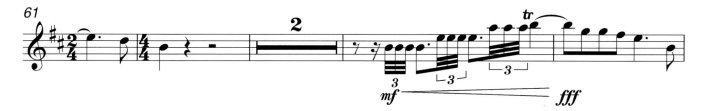

Alto Saxophone

Vocalise

Sergei Rachmaninov, Op. 34, No. 14
arr. G. Banaszak (1989)

Serenade

"Ständchen" from *Schwanengesang*

Franz Schubert, D957 No. 4
arr. G. Banaszak (1991)

MMO 4143

The printed piano accompaniment parts for the pieces in this album

(and Sax II part for First Light*)*

are available in pdf format

Please download these at

http://musicminusone.com/accompaniment/MMO4143/

username: MMO4143

password: M4143MO

For our full catalogue of saxophone releases, including popular and jazz titles, classical concerti, chamber works and master classes
visit us on the web at
www.musicminusone.com

50 Executive Blvd. • Elmsford, NY 10523
Call 1-800 669-7464 in the USA • 914 592-1188 International • Fax: 914 592-3575
email: info@musicminusone.com